Mag

MAGIC MIRROR

and other poems for children

Judith Nicholls

faber and faber

LONDON · BOSTON

First published in 1985
by Faber and Faber Limited
3 Queen Square London WC1N 3AU

Phototypeset by Wilmaset Birkenhead Merseyside
Printed in Great Britain by
Whitstable Litho Ltd Whitstable Kent

© Judith Nicholls, 1985

British Library Cataloguing in Publication Data

Nicholls, Judith
Magic mirror and other poems for children.
I. Title
821'.914   PR6064.I17/

ISBN 0–571–13696–6

Contents

For John,
Dominique, Guy and Tracey
with love

ALL ABOARD!

Hurry! cried Noah,
and into the ark
rushed

the osprey and the otter
the ostrich and the ox,
the jackal, kangaroo and kite
the scorpion and the fox.
The cacomistle, fresh from sleep
inside his hollow tree,
the cockroach and the cockatoo
the whistling chickadee.
The leopard and the tiger
the squat-nosed liverfluke,
the slow-worm and the glow-worm
and the shy young snake-eyed sheik.
Hinny, hippo, hobby,
hyena, hare and horse,
they all rushed over Noah's plank
before the storm broke loose.

Come in, come in! cried Noah,
Firefly, light these cloudy skies!
In crept grass-snake and glass-snake,
begging birds and mice.

Welcome mealybug and barnacle
and you too, leaf-nosed bat!
Do watch the step – our table's set,
the meal is steaming hot.
I only hope – these skies are black –
our simple ark won't fail!
The swan flew in disdainfully
with Chinese-painted quail.

Oh firefly, light our cloudy skies!
Do come in, mole and rat.
If God is willing, here's your home
beside Mount Ararat.

NIGHT

There's a dark, dark wood
inside my head
where the night owl cries;
where clambering roots
catch at my feet
where fox and bat
and badger meet
and night has eyes.

There's a dark, dark wood
inside my head
of oak and ash and pine;
where the clammy grasp
of a beaded web
can raise the hairs
on a wanderer's head
as he stares alone
from his mossy bed
and feels
the chill of his spine.

There's a dark, dark wood
inside my head
where the spider weaves;
where the rook rests
and the pale owl nests,
where moonlit bracken
spikes the air
and the moss is covered,
layer upon layer,
by a thousand fallen leaves.

FISHING SONG

Ragworm, lugworm, mackerel, maggot,
Grey pike lurking, still as steel.
Cast my rod in the deep dark stream
With a nugget of bread for a silver bream.
                              Caught an eel.

Ragworm, lugworm, mackerel, maggot,
Number Ten hook and I'm waiting still.
A carp would be good or a spiny perch,
A golden rudd or a red-finned roach?
                              It's an eel.

Ragworm, lugworm, mackerel, maggot,
Something's biting, wind up the reel!
Is it a pike or a roach or a rudd?
A hunting gudgeon from the river bed?
                              Just – an eel.

BALLAD OF THE SAD ASTRONAUT

Why are you weeping, child of the future,
For what are you grieving, son of the earth?
Acorns of autumn and white woods of winter,
Song-thrush of spring in the land of my birth.

You have a new life, child of the future,
Drifting through stars to a land of your own.
With Sirius to guide you, Orion beside you
Wandering the heavens you are free from earth's
harm.

I have a new life, the speckled skies' beauty,
Left far behind me the dark cries of earth;
Oh, but I long for the soft rains of April,
Ice-ferned Decembers and suns of the south.

What was I dreaming, to drift with Orion,
To leave for cold Neptune my home and my hearth?
Stars in their millions stretch endless, remind me
Far far behind lies my blue-marbled earth.

Here on the hillside the dawn is just rising,
Buttercups dew-fill, all silken and gold.
Well may you weep, sad child of the future,
Well may you yearn for your beautiful world.

MOONSCAPE

No air, no mist, no man, no beast.
No water flows from her Sea of Showers,
no trees, no flowers fringe her Lake of Dreams.
No grass grows or clouds shroud her high hills
or deep deserts. No whale blows in her dry
                              Ocean of Storms.

MIDAS

'The touch of gold!'
King Midas boldly craved.
Eyes glittered as he ran
from Bacchus' mountain cave
to find a golden land
where purple grape and twig of oak,
sleek lizard, stone and waving corn
like golden apples of the sun
all gilded to his stroke.

'A golden future!'
Midas cried
upon his golden throne.
And scarlet rose with olive branch,
plump aubergine and fragrant grass
passed through his grasping Judas kiss
to dazzle in the sun.

'Bring on the feast!'
King Midas laughed,
reached out for wine and bread;
raised his glass to take a sip
but when the red wine touched his lip
King Midas understood.

Oh gold was my corn and green my vine
and red was my wine of old;
never again shall I pine for wealth
or crave a richer world.

Lord Bacchus took pity, freed the king
from the gift he had longed to hold;
yet Autumn comes still with its Midas touch,
turns all to dying gold.

WORDHUNTER

My brother chases frogs –
well, eggs to be precise,
that jelly-baby spawn
which lurks near murky weed
after the winter's ice.
Takes them from the very doors
of hairy water-boatmen's jaws.
But me,
I'm a wordhunter.

Now my uncle,
he hunts butterflies.
Searches nettles, heaps of dung
for Purple Emperors, cabbage white,
Swallowtails with painted wing –
I'm sure you know the kind of thing.
Not me,
I'm a wordhunter.

See my sister Sue.
She chases – daydreams.
Laugh or tease, she just replies
'What do I care?'
Closes eyes and quickly flies
back to her castles in the air.
Not me,
I'd rather be

                        A WORDHUNTER.

There's wiggle and giggle
goggles and swatch,
straggle and gaggle
and toggle and itch.

Glimmering, shimmering,
glistening, twinkle,
poppycock, puddle
and muddle and pimple.

Peapod and flip-flop,
rickety, dodo,
murmuring, lingering,
galaxy, yo-yo.

Extra-terrestrial's
one that I love,
Betelgeuse, Pluto –
Heavens above!

Who would not fall
for a bird called a chickadee?
A widgeon or warthog
or just the old chimpanzee?

Many's the word
that I capture each day,
whispering each
till I know it will stay.

Safely they sit
in my wordhunter's store –
and when I feel hungry
I wordhunt for more.

JONAH

Jonah was a later one
among God's prophets,
not one to be sat upon,
didn't do as asked;
you could even say, alas,
he was rather like a
naughty little boy!
Off you go to Nineveh,
said God one day, Your task
to tell them that
I know about their
wickedness. In forty days
I shall destroy.

So did our Jonah move?
No.
He thought along these lines:
God is loving, he'll forgive,
give a second chance, let live.
Will He really kill?
I don't believe He will!
They'll all think I've gone mad,
I *won't* do as He says,
it really is too bad!

So off he went,
but not to Nineveh;
caught a boat for Spain in
Jaffa's port. Can you blame him?

Out at sea,
the storm began.
Full of fear and shaking to a man,
the sailors, terrified, began to pray.
Jonah slept.
Pray, the captain cried.
What can I say, cried Jonah in dismay.
God sent this storm because I ran away.
Throw me overboard, said Jonah,
then the loving Lord, said Jonah,
will sooth the savage seas.
And all the sailors wept.

At last they threw him over in alarm,
watched in wonder as the angry seas grew calm.
Every sailor and his captain out of harm
now gave a prayer of thanks to this new God.
But what of Jonah?

The grey waves rose over him,
the wild waves closed over him,
he called to God for help.
Yes, his Lord had followed him,
sent a fish which swallowed him!
Safe inside the whale he wallowed in
despair.

Alone, afraid and sad,
for three dark days he stayed
inside the murky cavern of the whale.
Jonah thought;
wished he never had
ignored his only God,
felt it wrong he'd been
so mad and said,
well – sorry, Lord.
Would he live to tell his sorry tale?

At last the time was come.
With a wriggle and a shlurp
and a tidal wave of burp
the whale now cast out
Jonah on a beach.
With danger out of reach
he thanked the Lord for sun.

Straight away
he went to Nineveh,
took the message to the people,
and the people, they believed;
changed their ways so utterly
that God did not destroy them
and – can you guess? – Yes!
Jonah felt aggrieved.

Sat down outside the city,
moaned he'd known
what God would do; gave a sigh
half full of anger, half self-pity,
asked God now to leave him there to die.

God said no.
Sent a plant to grow
and shade him from the desert sun,
made him feel much better yet again.
But then
             next day
                     the plant
                             began
                                   to die.

I liked that plant,
said Jonah, sad; I'm
sorry that it's gone.
I may seem just a moaner, but
I just don't understand.
You are sorry for a plant,
I was sorry for a nation
that I'd given life, said God.
I saw that in their fashion
they had learnt.

And Jonah,
head in hand
on that gold and burning sand
began to think,
began to feel,
began to see.

At last, he said, I think I understand.

ANDROMEDA

On a mole-black night when the stars are bright
And the cloud-veiled moon is high,
If you search near the wings of Pegasus
You can see her in the sky.

Chained fast to a rock, she waits her fate
As the great sea-monster's prey;
As she hides in fear she can hear the hiss
Of Cetus on his way.

But wait, it's the swish of Pegasus' wings
With Perseus riding high!
On a mole-black night with the stars in flight
You can see them ride away.

UNCLE WILLIAM

I stayed with you once
in your tiny church-lane cottage
with the outside pump, the velvet cloth
and sing-songs cramped around the piano.

With black-fringed stumps of fingers,
braces, ample paunch,
you could have been
miner, dustman, sweep –
but no; village blacksmith
fitted best that village scene.

I remember strong green soap,
tin bowls of icy water for the morning wash;
my aunt's night-calling for the cat
across still hedgerows and the cobbled lane,
a shared bed with spoiling cousins,
Billy Bunter by oil lamp at forbidden hours
and orange moths against the darkened pane.

Uncle William. Dead now;
the blacksmith and the cottage gone.
No cobbled lane but just a road now,
a road my aunt must tread alone.

DREAM OF THE FAIR FOREST

Where can I hide in you,
forest, fair forest?
Where can I hide in you,
forest so green?

Hide in my pine trees,
my beeches, my aspen.
Hide in my maples,
where none can be seen.

How shall I live in you,
forest, fair forest?
How shall I live in you,
forest so gay?

Live on my berries,
my cobnuts, my rosehips.
Live on my blackberries,
they'll last many-a-day.

Who shall I live with,
oh forest, fair forest?
Who shall I live with,
my forest so wild?

Live with my squirrels,
my nuthatch, my night owls.
Live with my badgers
and live as my child.

What shall I lie on,
green forest, my forest?
What shall I lie on
when night starts to fall?

Lie on my grasses,
my rosebay, my lichen.
Lie on my mosses,
the softest of all.

What if I'm lonely,
fine forest, fair forest?
What if I dream
of returning to town?

You won't be lonely,
fair dreamchild, my wanderer.
With fox cub and grey dove
you won't be alone.

POMPEII

24th August, A.D. 79

The giants are sleeping now
under a hot land
where the grey snow
has yet to fall
and cover all
with its dying dew.

The city is silent now
under a haze of blue
till the pedlar's cart
on the stone-clad street
calls the early few
for pot or shoe
and the slave from sleep.

The hillside is sunwashed now
where the lush vine
and the olives line
the summer slopes
of the giants' home
in an August dream
that has almost gone.

The gods are sleeping now
unaware
by the temple walls
and market stalls
of the city square . . .

And an ashen cloud
shrouds the breathless crowd
as the grey snow falls.

SUNFLOWER

guards my south wall,
a private sun.
Floodlights the whole garden,
warms tardy flowerbeds into life
in leafy July.

She turns to face the sun – we're told;
I know it's wrong.
Really the sun chases my Inca goddess,
jealous of rival gold.

LATE

You're late, said miss.
The bell has gone,
dinner numbers done
and work begun.

What have you got to say for yourself?

Well, it's like this, miss.
Me mum was sick,
me dad fell down the stairs,
the wheel fell off me bike
and then we lost our Billy's snake
behind the kitchen chairs. Earache
struck down me grampy, me gran
took quite a funny turn.
Then on the way I met this man
whose dog attacked me shin –
look, miss, you can see the blood,
it doesn't look too good,
does it?

Yes, yes, sit down –
and next time say you're sorry
for disturbing all the class.
Now get on with your story,
fast!

Please miss, I've got nothing to write about.

SCHOOL DINNERS

The greater-spotted brown baked bean's
not quite the humble bird it seems;
it lurks beneath the soggy greens
                   waiting to get you.

The green unruly jumping pea
has no respect for you or me;
it's bound to land on miss's knee
                   and she'll get you.

The brown-backed flying liverslug
is little better than a thug;
you think you're safe – don't be too smug
                   he'll get you.

The quiet skulking greasychip
looks innocent – that's just his trick;
eat thirds or fourths and you'll be sick
                   he'll get you.

The many-fingered crumb-y fish
looks friendly, as you might well wish;
but leave him lying on your dish
                   he'll get you.

TEACHER SAID . . .

You can use
    mumbled and muttered,
    groaned, grumbled and uttered,
    professed, droned or stuttered
        . . . but *don't* use SAID!

You can use
    rant or recite,
    yell, yodel or snort,
    bellow, murmur or moan,
    you can grunt or just groan
        . . . but *don't* use SAID!

You can
    hum, howl and hail,
    scream, screech, shriek or bawl,
    squeak, snivel or squeal
    with a blood-curdling wail
        . . . but *don't* use SAID!

        . . . SAID my teacher.

LINES

I must never daydream in schooltime.
I just love a daydream in Mayshine.
I must ever greydream in timeschool.
Why must others paydream in schoolway?
Just over highschool dismay lay.
Thrust over skydreams in cryschool.
Cry dust over drydreams in screamtime.
Dreamschool thirst first in dismayday.
Why lie for greyday in crimedream?
My time for dreamday is soontime.
In soontime must I daydream ever.
Never must I say dream in strifetime.
Cry dust over daydreams of lifetimes.
I must never daydream in schooltime.
In time I must daydream never.

SPACE-SHUTTLE

Monday
my Aunt Esmeralda
gave me one of those
s p a c e – h o p p e r s .
You know,
those big orange things
that you sit on and
they're supposed to take you to the s t a r s
Didn't take me any further than
the lamp-post –
and that hurt.

Tuesday
I gave it to my baby brother.
Do you know, he really believes
it's going to work!
Some people will believe
anything.

Friday.
Just had a postcard
from my brother.
From the moon.
It says
'Had a good journey.
See you soon.
Just hopping off to M a r s !'

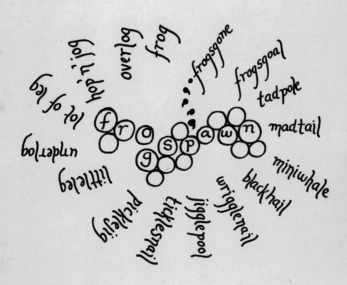

SNOW IN DECEMBER

Old willow fur-draped
against the winds; stars shiver
in a cool grey sky.

MAGIC MIRROR

Step before the magic mirror,
tell me what you see?

Could it be
    me, stretched tall,
    unfolded, gaudy blanket,
    giant transfer
    ironed to the wall,
    a sprawl of paint
    splashed in a dull hall
    by a lonely stair?

Could it be
    some painted circus clown
    blown from a nearby town,
    oil, marbled in a puddle,
    fuddled stained-glass window,
    Joseph's coloured coat,
    or splintered light
    from Noah's rainbow,
    low in a torn grey sky,
    after the storm?

Could it be
    Christmas crackers
    in wrappers tinselled
    and bright as a glass bauble,
    a summer garden
    dancing through rainy glass,
    waving flags, each one
    flown for a fair princess,
    or trembling wings
    of dragonflies,
    caught in August sun?

You look in the magic mirror,
tell me what you see;
is that really only – me?

JAPHETH'S NOTES: A FRAGMENT

Blue wash
drifting to grey.
First waterdrops
on father's up-turned head,
dew on a web of thinning hair.
Mist gathers over Ararat.

Voices of man and animal
up-pitched by fear.
Hammers drum a crescendo.
Plaintive duo of wolves howl
their elegy for drowning world.
Waters rise over Ararat.

Nostrils sharp with
gopherwood and pitch,
damp fur and panic-sweat.
Paws and claws jostle,
trail mud and excrement.
Sweet-sour smell
of ripening oranges,
fermenting grape
and olive oil.
Lord, may we safely
sink to earth on Ararat.

THEN

They never expected it of my grandmother,
all this choice.
Stolid, vocationally-trained
with neat samplers and clear instructions on
pastry-making and how to preserve the strawberries,
for forty years she happily baked my grandfather
rabbit pie, brawn, haslet;
collected fresh farm milk,
still-twitching pullets
and their warm muck-splattered eggs,
manure for the rhubarb, and mushrooms
dawn-gathered in chill Lincolnshire fields.

STABLE SONG

She lies, a stillness in the crumpled straw
Whilst he looks softly on the child, unsure,
And shadows waver by the stable door.

The oxen stir; a moth drifts through the bare
Outbuilding, silken Gabriel-winged, to where
She lies, a stillness in the crumpled straw.

A carpenter, his wife, both unaware
That kings and shepherds seek them from afar
And shadows waver by the stable door.

The child sleeps on. A drowse of asses snore;
He murmurs gently, raises eyes to her
Who lies, a stillness in the crumpled straw.

A cockerel crows, disturbed by sudden fear
As shepherds, dark upon the hill, appear
And shadows waver by the stable door.

The hush of birth is in the midnight air
And new life hides the distant smell of myrrh;
She lies, a stillness in the crumpled straw,
And shadows waver by the stable door.

REPORT

They said me grammar
wasn't too good.
She were all right
when I seed her last week.

He must learn to speak
proper, they said.
What cheek –
I can speak!
They should be glad
I'm there at all.

His sums ain't bad
though he has trouble
with his tables,
they said.

Me dad says
not to worry, lad.
Tables is for eatin' off,
he says.

Who's for a jam butty?

SEA SONG

Come sail the whispering seas, my love,
Come drift on the tides with me;
For I still long for the wild waves' song
And the silver fish of the sea.

Oh I'd sail the sighing seas, my love,
Where the wild weeds gently glide;
But I'm afraid of the forest shade
Where the silent fishes hide.

Don't fear the sauntering seas, my love,
As they dance beneath the breeze;
In the moonlit foam we'll make our home
Like the silver fish of the seas.

Oh I'll sail the rolling seas, my love,
And sigh for the cry of the wind;
But what if I weep on the ocean deep
To tread a greener land?

Oh you'll love the roaring seas, my love!
Come ride the swell with me,
Where the breaking sky is drawn to die
With the silver fish of the sea.

If I ride the raging seas, my love,
Then will you follow me?
Or will you stay till your dying day
With the silver fish of the sea?

Oh I must ride the wild, wild seas
And you must let me be;
Till my dying day I'll roam the spray
With the silver fish of the sea.

SPIDER'S SONG

See, I have stitched the ivy
with beaded threads of light,
a rich embroidery, newly hung.
Step on my tightrope,
lie with me;
let me fold you tenderly
in my pearled hammock,
lull you to silken sleep,
sweet dreamer,
under the dying sun.

MOSES – a sequence

SEARCHER

Princess, what are you dreaming,
down among the moist rushes?

Soft pleated linen, beaded bracelets,
purple grapes and Pharaoh's finest wines
await you at the palace –

yet you follow
a wavering baby's cry.

PLEASE, PHARAOH!

Pharaoh,
what use your
flutes and lutes now,
your bronze mirrors and
dancing girls in beaded anklets?

Locusts
have blackened
your figs, your corn
for bread, your dates and
grapes and pomegranates. Your crops

and rich
cattle dead,
river turned to
blood; for what good? Which
god will you call on now? And how?

A QUESTION OF PLAGUE

Pharaoh,
how do you like
frogs in your bed, locusts
gorging corn, boils too raw to touch?
Not much!

PLAGUE FROG

I am
  the frog
    that leapt
      from the Nile
        that hopped
          to the palace
            that flipped
              to the bedroom
              that slipped
                in the sheet
                that flopped
                  with a smile
                  then nipped
                  at the feet
                    of the king who
                      kept Moses in Egypt.

COME ON, MOSES!

Sing to the Lord,
sang Miriam,
took her tambourine;
you've never seen
dances of such joy.
Soon after, hunger
erased the memory of
slave-drivers and whips,
Egyptian bosses, bricks
they ordered with no straw
offered, as many as before.
Hunger conjured onions,
crinkly cucumbers, melons
once enjoyed each day.
Someone had to pay,
and why not Moses?

Better die in Egypt, they cried
than lie in this desert, burn
in parching sun. Rather turn
again to Pharaoh. At least
we were fed. Maybe not free
but not dead either. Water, food!
Fetch us drink and find our bread!
Come on, Moses! Where's this god?